The Ought

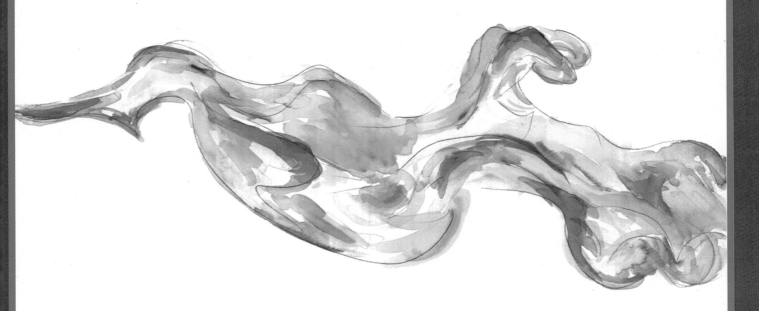

By Prof. Wiz
Illustrated by Renae Dower

To order additional copies of this book, contact:
Xlibris LLC
1-888-795-4274
www.Xlibris.com
Orders@Xlibris.com

The Ought

By Prof. Wiz
Illustrated by Renae Dower

What is The Ought?

What is around us, in us, and tells us what needs to be done?
"You ought to do this. You ought not do that." That's The Ought.

Nobody wants to hear "You ought…" because it grabs us, directs us, and forms us. — We think it takes away our freedom.

PROF. WIZ

So nobody likes The Ought.

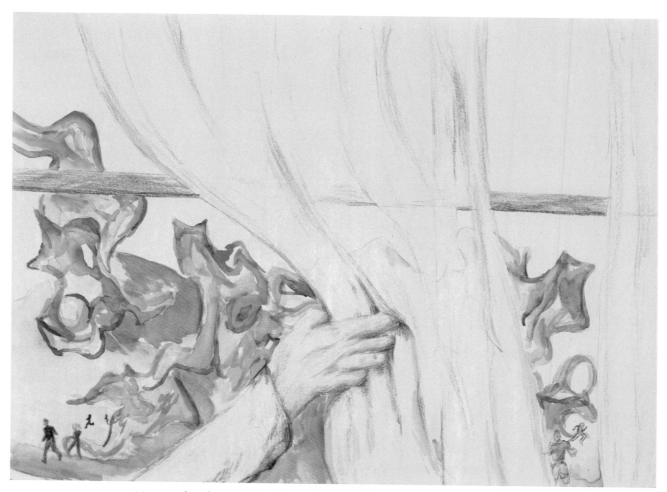

Not only do we dislike The Ought, we are afraid of it.
When The Ought comes everybody runs. — We even deny it exists.

When we feel its presence we think, "How can The Ought be real for you and me, when we are so different and see the world so differently? We each have our own oughts. There is no Ought, but only our own personal oughts."

So we convince ourselves that there is no Ought (we think someone made it up). In its place we put our own pet, personal oughts (that take the form of wishes).

But they are not the real animal, because oughts we choose are not The Ought that chooses us.

We say (with regards to Dr. Seuss):

"The Ought can't choose me because that would form me.
I can only be informed, not transformed."

And we say:

"The Ought can't form me because it is too late.
I have already been formed by friends and family, and shaped in my home state."

But how can we say both, "The Ought can't form me because I am already formed," and, "The Ought can't form me because that would form me"?

We want so much to believe that The Ought doesn't make sense, we make excuses that don't make sense. We want so much to believe it isn't real, we say things that are unreal.

If it were really nothing (a naught, not The Ought), we could ignore it—like a ghost in the closet.

But we can't.

We try to avoid The Ought. We hear its voice, yet close our ears.
We feel its touch, yet cover up.

The Ought is real. It grabs us, directs us, and forms us.
That's why we fear it, flee from it, and even deny it exists.

So where does The Ought come from? Can we find The Ought?

When we search for The Ought, when we consider the things that we should and shouldn't do, we bring together our own ideas, our common sense, and our best judgment too.

We see that everyone who searches for The Ought is important. They have ideas, they have feelings, they have will power, and they deserve respect.

Then do you know what we discover? We find that The Ought finds us.

We understand that everyone ought to be treated in certain ways, including ourselves.
This gives us dignity, and frees us to respect others.

Then we see The Ought.

So we need not fear The Ought, though we will be awed by it.

For The Ought has the power to grab our minds to think honestly, form our hearts to feel sympathetically, and direct our wills to act rightly.

The Ought is us.

Printed in the United States
by Baker & Taylor Publisher Services